T0376349

Praise for *Soul Friend and Other Love Notes to the Natural World*

Reading Sheila McEntee's collection of essays is the literary equivalent of what the Japanese call "forest bathing." In unhurried, lyrical language, she guides us through landscapes—and lifescapes—with the intimacy and generosity of a best friend.

Soul Friend is a book about nature, but also about human nature. Woven with her observations of birds and wildflowers are explorations of personal-but-universal joys and griefs; gifts and losses; loneliness; love; and flashes of spiritual grace that, like a winter flock of cardinals, alight for a moment and leave a memory for a lifetime.

Savor these essays, reader. You will be well rewarded to follow McEntee as she leads you, flower by fern by birdcall, along a path "like a cathedral aisle, green boughs meeting high overhead in a holy embrace."

Colleen Anderson, author of
Bound Stone and *Missing: Mrs. Cornblossom*

Good writing—and good living—stem from slowing down and paying attention. Sheila McEntee's essay collection *Soul Friend* invites us to do just that through her vivid encounters with birds and bears, loneliness and longing, family and friendship. There is joy in this writing, a joy that arises not only out of ease but also pain, not only out of light but also darkness. This makes each crystalline moment of recognition McEntee frames for us that much more powerful, a meditative practice bearing witness to what's already there around and within us, asking for relationship. Read this book and watch and wait. You may be surprised at your own soul's voice calling you forward.

Jonathan Callard, award-winning writer and teacher
(jonathancallard.com)

In her collection of essays, Sheila McEntee guides the reader through the complex, inspiring, and curious natural world in which we live. What makes her collection so accessible, though, is her ability to allow us to see ourselves in that world, not just as observers of the natural processes or inhabitants of that world, but as participants, who can learn from those observations. The opposite of anthropomorphizing, her work uses the lives and process we see all around us as a tool of enlightenment, asking us to reflect on our experiences of joy, loss, and wonder, triggered by those observations. At their core, these essays serve as a meditation for self-reflection and appreciation for the world around us. A welcome respite from the hurry-scurry of the virtual world we spend much of our time inhabiting.

Curtis Smalling, Vice President,
Audubon North Carolina

Soul Friend and Other Love Notes to the Natural World is a poignant blend of natural history and personal reminiscences. It will find avid readers in professional field naturalists and serious bird-watchers, as well as casual backyard observers. From a touching piece on the death of her mother to stories of amusing animal antics in her own backyard, the book had me remembering, laughing, and simply enjoying Sheila's take on the natural world.

Scott Shalaway,
certified wildlife biologist, syndicated columnist,
and author of *Building a Backyard Bird Habitat*

With poetic grace, keen insights on the human condition, and a clear reverence for the natural world, McEntee crafts her essays with a sensitivity reminiscent of Mary Oliver and a nimbleness evocative of Joan Didion. Each essay unfolds like a prayer, a testament to the fragile interconnectedness of all living beings. I adored every moment of *Soul Friend*, and you will, too.

Nora Shalaway Carpenter, award-winning author of
The Edge of Anything and *Fault Lines*

Sheila McEntee's wonderful collection of essays weaves an exploratory narrative of people, memory, and place, with West Virginia's natural abundance at its heart.

Merging lyrical prose with research, she illuminates how the state's diverse birdlife serves as a symbol of both personal and spiritual inspiration, and ecological health. Perhaps most importantly, her work highlights the great value, and challenge, in experiencing the moment-to-moment immediacy of nature—increasingly a deficit in our modern lives. Accordingly, this book is recommended reading for anyone looking to reconnect with themselves and the surrounding world.

Richard S. Bailey, State Ornithologist,
West Virginia Division of Natural Resources

The beauty of Sheila McEntee's collection of essays, *Soul Friend*, is that she leads the gentle way into slowing down, watching and listening to the natural world around her, and incorporating the ebb and flow of the seasons into daily life. It is a naturalist's interaction on a spiritual and practical level, tying human life with the natural world. Birds are integral to the mix, often easing the transition from the immediate into contemplation of the whole. *Soul Friend* is a thoughtful collection that leaves the reader with a more complete view of our natural world, inviting the reader to go explore the outdoors.

Wendy Perrone, Executive Director,
Three Rivers Avian Center

Sheila McEntee has a deep connection to, and appreciation for, the natural world, whether she is walking in the woods or looking out her kitchen window. A keen, patient observer, she finds details in nature that others overlook and reveals them to the reader in elegant prose that borders on the poetic. Her stories are profound, poignant, and moving, drawing from the birds and other creatures insights that resonate deeply with our human experience.

Daniel Day, www.jerseybirder.com

Soul Friend
and Other Love Notes
to the Natural World

SHEILA MCENTEE

A Blackwater Press book

First published in the United States of America by
Blackwater Press, LLC

Copyright © Sheila McEntee, 2025

Library of Congress Control Number: 2025930304

ISBN: 978-1-963614-09-1

Illustrated by Sophie Kromholz

Blackwater Press
120 Capitol Street
Charleston, WV 25301
United States

blackwaterpress.com

All that I hope to say in books, all that I ever hope to say, is that I love the world.
—E. B. White

TABLE OF CONTENTS

For my father, Jack McEntee, who taught me to love birds, and for my grandfather, Edward C. McEntee, who said, "You should write."

Preface

I CAUGHT this morning morning's minion, kingdom of daylight's dauphin, dapple-dawn-drawn Falcon, in
     his riding
Of the rolling level underneath him steady air,...

In the spring of 1976, in a Modern British Poetry class
at the College of the Holy Cross, I discovered "The
Windhover: To Christ Our Lord" by Jesuit poet Gerard
Manley Hopkins. My professor pointed out Hopkins's
masterful use of alliteration and assonance, and the
way he chose words to create the movements of a falcon riding air currents across the sky:

                            ... and striding
High there, how he rung upon the rein of a wimpling wing
In his ecstasy! then off, off forth on swing,
  As a skate's heel sweeps smooth on a bow-bend: the hurl and
     gliding
  Rebuffed the big wind. My heart in hiding
Stirred for a bird,—the achieve of, the mastery of the
thing!...

The poem took my breath away. Right then and there, I fell in love with a falcon in flight and with Hopkins's poetry.

Later, in my junior year, I was thrilled to take a class devoted solely to Hopkins's works with just a handful of other students. Where else but at a small, Jesuit college could I have pursued my newfound passion in so intimate a setting and in such depth? Together with the Reverend William Van Etten Casey, SJ, we further explored Hopkins's use of particular words and poetic techniques to express what the poet called *inscape*, or the very essence of natural things: the sea, the stars, the song of a thrush, a chestnut, even weeds. In all of these things Hopkins found not only beauty but the presence of God. In studying his poems deeply, I grew to admire not only his extraordinary gift for language but also his profound presence to the natural world, where he always saw the Divine.

Some years after graduating from Holy Cross, I moved to West Virginia, a hilly, sparsely populated state with more than a million acres of public woodlands, wetlands, and other natural areas. As my family and I discovered hiking and camping in the forests of Appalachia, my reverence for nature grew, and my connection to Gerard Manley Hopkins was renewed.

I remember sitting on the curb of our cul-de-sac, watching my small children play, and looking up to see a dark, majestic bird circling in the sky, gently tilting from side to side, deftly riding the autumn air currents. "The Windhover" immediately sprang to mind. I later learned that the bird, with its gray flight feathers and fingerlike wingtips, was not a falcon but a turkey vulture. Yet, knowing this in no way diminished my joy and awe in watching its ecstatic flight.

Since that moment, Hopkins's deep reverence for the natural world has been a touchstone for me in my outdoor explorations and my writing. He reminds me to be attentive, to pause and listen to the whinnies and chortles of an American robin, to the chuckling of a white-breasted nuthatch. I think of him when I bend to admire the creamy-white petals of bloodroot, or the crimson cup of wild ginger, hiding beneath broad, spade-shaped leaves. He is there when I touch the soft fronds of a maidenhair fern; the deep, rough furrows of a black walnut tree; and the smooth, cool bark of a beech.

Long ago, my father taught me to love birds by showing me how to feed and identify the ones who visited our backyard. But it wasn't until I moved to West Virginia that I learned that the forest is filled with brilliantly colored warblers in spring, and that if you listen closely, you can identify a bird by its voice without seeing it at all. Over the years, naturalist friends also showed me that Appalachian woodlands are a riot of color from spring to fall, as myriad wildflowers, from diminutive bluets to tall, yellow wingstem, rise up and bloom, each in its own time.

Now, though I relish a solitary walk in the woods with my dog, I am never truly alone. Always by my side are the many teachers who so generously shared their passion for nature with me.

I like to think of these essays, which span some twenty years, as love notes to the natural world. They are also grateful tributes to those who woke me to its beauty and healing power. This book honors my home state of West Virginia as well. After thirty-five years, I can no longer imagine living anywhere where refuge on a quiet, mostly unpeopled trail is more than a few minutes away. I have come to rely deeply on the wild nature of my home, not only for inspiration and recreation, but also for communion and comfort.

FROM POETRY TO PROSE

Though I am an essayist, not a poet, I recently discovered that esteemed poet Billy Collins and I have much in common. For one, we both love words. For another, we are fellow alums of Holy Cross, a small, Jesuit, liberal arts college in Worcester, Massachusetts. Third (and coolest of all), we both write haikus while walking our dogs. For Billy, it is a practical way to practice his art. For me, it is an avenue to awareness and to deepening my prose.

I've never met Billy Collins, but I know about his poetic promenades because he mentions them in his introduction to *Haiku in English: The First Hundred Years*. Billy says he first discovered haiku in high school, when he was just beginning to explore Beat literature and Zen sensibilities. He dabbled in it a bit but then gave it up, considering his works "unwitting travesties to the ancient and honorable tradition."

Decades later, he rediscovered the form after he rescued a dog from the local animal shelter. A mixed-breed female, he named her Jeannine, after a Cannonball Adderley tune. Billy and Jeannine take long, daily walks around a reservoir, she sniffing and he counting syllables on his fingers. He tries to return home each day with a new haiku.

"I like to think of the haiku as a moment-smashing device out of which arise powerful moments of dazzling awareness," Billy writes. "But I also like to think of it as something to do while walking the dog."

I was both affirmed and delighted when I read about Billy's haiku dog walking, for I had begun the same practice some months before. My loyal companions, Murphy and Missy, and I log many miles together, walking in our densely residential neighborhood. The dogs never fail to find fascinating scents, while I muse on countless haiku-worthy subjects, some of which find their way into my prose. Like Billy, I stick to the 5-7-5 syllable structure, counting them out on my fingers.

Most mornings, it is all too clear that the pups and I have different agendas:

> Brisk walk or sniffing
> expedition? Ever a
> negotiation.

Here's one from a moment in deep summer, when I was especially delighted to hear the light, lilting flute song of my favorite bird. The wood thrush and its captivating voice have appeared in my nature writing time and again:

> July morning, baked
> air too thick to breathe, and yet,
> a wood thrush singing

Here is a lonely image I discovered on a recent winter walk:

At the tips of bare
branches, a tiny bowl of
twigs long abandoned

When I attempt to write a haiku while walking with Murphy and Missy, I begin my day with a small stab at creativity. I like the idea of preserving an image, a moment, that would otherwise have gone unnoticed. I also like being fully present to something. As Billy says, a haiku declares "that someone was present—actually there, living and breathing—at that particular intersection of sight and sound."

The gentle gathering of ordinary moments is important to me as a writer. It keeps my mind stoked and attuned to the world around me. It also gives me a feeling of accomplishment. I sometimes think, "If I write nothing else today, I have recorded this." My haiku collection has since become a sort of poetic diary.

When I get home, I quickly scribble down my haikus before I forget them. Often I marvel at their brilliance. Days later, I come back to them and see that they are clunky and utilitarian—indeed, "unwitting travesties." Sometimes I refine them. Most times I let them be. I won't enter them in a contest. It's unlikely I'd publish them in a book, though I once used some of my better ones to introduce the sections of a segmented essay. In any case, they remain evidence of sweet moments I'd have otherwise missed or forgotten.

Of course, composing haikus can happen anywhere: on the subway, in the car, at the DMV. No need to be an esteemed poet, and no one will notice your gentle finger counting. You just have to remember to write them down, for

they vanish quickly,
like dreams, or dew, or wisps of
fog in morning light.

Selving

As kingfishers catch fire, dragonflies draw flame;
As tumbled over rim in roundy wells
Stones ring; like each tucked string tells, each hung bell's
Bow swung finds tongue to fling out broad its name;
Each mortal thing does one thing and the same:
Deals out that being indoors each one dwells;
Selves—goes itself; *myself* it speaks and spells,
Crying *What I do is me: for that I came....*
—*Gerard Manley Hopkins, SJ*

As kingfishers catch fire, dragonflies draw flame;

On a Sunday morning in spring, I wrap chilled fingers, one newly bare of adornment, around the smooth steering wheel of my car and drive to a place where most people do not gather to pray. As I begin the descent from Connell Road to Loudendale, to the fringes of Kanawha State Forest, Seamus, lying still on the seat beside me, raises his head lazily and begins to sniff. Below half-closed eyes, his snout gently bobs in the air, as if something vaguely familiar has caught his attention. With each mile we drive, Seamus grows more alert, and his sniffing intensifies. By the time we reach the entrance to the forest, he is sitting erect, front legs stiff—taut with excitement—straining to read the air streaming through the vents and the tops of the windows. He is intoxicated with memory. Fur abristle, his body nearly pulsates with the thought of what is to come. He knows he will soon be unleashed—free to bound up rocky trails, leap over gullies, traipse into creeks—belly fur cooled, wet, and muddy. To squat in the leaves—who cares where? To mark any tree. To dig. To ferret out. Like a practiced hurdler to leap over felled, decaying trees. But most of all, to run and run and run out his pent up, often denied dogness. He will race ahead of me, barreling in near flight, broad feet beating the path, toenails scratching up earth, ruffling leaves, brown eyes bright orbs—wild—seeing past me, honoring a longing.

As tumbled over rim in roundy wells
Stones ring;

The path is like a cathedral aisle, green boughs meeting high overhead in a holy embrace. Like me, box turtle plods up the path. Scaled, sharp-nailed, splayed legs reach, slowly, one then the other, like a labored swimmer in a dry pool. Directed by an internal compass it goes forth, neck outstretched, black eyes forward, never shrinking. It knows no other way. We are tethered to the ground, box turtle and I, while zebra swallowtail—newly born—flits from tender leaves in constant motion, then settles but for a moment in a patch of sunlight to flex and dry freshly unfurled wings.

I find tall and bloody-red jack-in-the-pulpit, ordained forest preacher, elegant in his striped vestments. Foam-flower, with its columns of delicate bubbles, are the trailside faithful, as are the May apple blooms—those white-petaled starbursts—that worship privately beneath broad umbrella leaves.

Like that of the choir soloist, the voice of hooded warbler rises from a nearby thicket—above chickadee, nuthatch, even blue jay's blare. I close my eyes and listen for the flutist, but there is none this morning. Has wood thrush set aside his song to tend to his mate, to quietly help bring about birth?

like each tucked string tells, each hung bell's
Bow swung finds tongue to fling out broad its name;

All black and prickle-haired you light upon my page, my pen, and then to the protruding knuckle of my thumb. Lacy filigree wings alert you tamp-tamp-tamp the damp skin of my finger with your proboscis, assessing me. Without insistent buzz or bite to distract me, I note your minute ensemble—shoes, like bright yellow mini-galoshes, to match your saucer eyes and the knobs of your antennae. You ride my thumb as blue words stream across a white page. Not intimidated by my size you tamp-tamp-touch—explore unafraid. I allow this for as long as you require. I am, after all, the visitor in this kingdom.

"Your flyness," I say, gently bowing my head.

Each mortal thing does one thing and the same:
Deals out that being indoors each one dwells;

That night I lie on the left side of the bed, the right side newly empty but also recently occupied with several days' worth of clothes, and an ever-increasing pile of books that attempt to explain the inner workings of the mind—the heart—and what dreams mean. The pages are bent back, some passages nearly committed to memory. They sport highlighter, underlining, purple tabs, asterisks sprinkled in the margins. Also amid them are a book or two that offer an escape into the made-up lives of others.

Some nights I wake to find Seamus curled against the backs of my knees. This night, before turning off the light, I watch him, his closed eyes, paws, and whiskered lips atwitter, the forest calling him again in sleep. For me, sleep comes in seconds and I, too, surrender to the will of my dreams:

The darkness of the forest is enveloping, like a warm shroud, but not altogether benign. I am alone, not expecting to be otherwise, and I have come, quite naturally, to the large wooden picnic shelter to do my laundry. A soft light emanates from the ceiling of the shelter.

As I walk purposefully toward the laundry room, carrying

nothing, I accidentally knock a box off the mantle of the shelter fireplace. Looking behind me, I see that the upset box holds a black, plastic trash bag. Suddenly, amid the sound of crinkling plastic, a small dinosaur—pink and round-backed with erect back fins— emerges from the bag. With growing alarm, I watch as the creature leaves the box and walks toward the laundry room.

"It's getting away," I think to myself, "and I can't put it back because I will not pick up a dinosaur. I cannot touch it."

Just then, I look down to see a second dinosaur emerge from the bag, this one smaller with softer, pinker skin. It, too, leaves the box, following its older companion. When I pick up the bag and peer inside, I find it teeming with slugs. They are brown, seeping en masse, united in their ooze. I drop the bag and turn away. I know that the box was left in the shelter for safekeeping. I feel I must somehow reach its owner, but how? There is no identification on it, and besides, I do not have my cell phone. And even if I did, it does not work in the forest. There is no signal. I stand limp in the dim light of the shelter, surrounded by night, feeling helpless and utterly responsible.

* * *

The South Side Bridge no longer exists. Did it crumble and fall away, or was it destroyed by terrorists? I do not know. I stand beside what is left, a mass of gray rubble. Now, above the river, sea birds fly through the great, gaping abyss.

* * *

My office holds an air of excitement this day. The table in the common area is set with a cake and red punch in a crystal bowl with matching cups. The women sit together in a circle. Everyone is smiling, talking softly, waiting for me to join them, for I am the guest of honor and this is a baby shower. Miraculously, I have just given birth, but no one would guess it. I have gained neither an inch nor a pound. In fact, my body has not changed in the slightest. I look the same. My friends look at me admiringly. "How did you do it?" they all want to know. I am pleased by their attentiveness, though baffled myself about how this came to be.

Selves—goes itself; *myself* it speaks and spells,
Crying *What I do is me; for that I came.*

Daffodil stems are freshest, most tender closest to the earth. They grow tall and dark with age, with time. Humble buds, heads bowed, almost serpentine, await the sun.

But are not the daffodil blooms themselves most beautiful? Full-fledged petals grace fluted tubes of deep, deep knowing, calling every year to a brief season from cores buried in the ground.

Soul Friend

One late summer morning, on my way to the river to swim, I find a dead bird, soaked and limp, lying at the water's edge. The gentle, lapping surf rocks its body to and fro.

It is a small bird by river standards. Not an eagle or osprey. Not even a gull, or cormorant, or crow. No, this bird is petite, robin-sized. Its body seems out of place so near the water.

"How did you get here, dear soul?" I ask the bird, as if its spirit, lingering lightly on the breeze, might answer me.

Bending to look more closely, I note that the bird's jet-black wings have white spots. Beneath them its legs extend stiff and straight, like mini matchsticks, ending in four curled toes. Two empty eye sockets stare blankly from its wet, bobbing head.

As I search for more clues to the bird's identity, the back of its head gives me a good one: I see a bright red patch, like a splotch of warm blood, beneath the clear, cold water. And then, the bird's bill tells me the rest: it is hefty and nearly as long as its head.

I know this bird now. He was not a creature of the water but of the tall pines and hardwoods. In life he was reclusive, not one to dally in the dramas of romping river life. The open, lapping surf, exposed to sun and wind, was not a fitting place for the story of a male hairy woodpecker to end.

Though I now know the bird's identity, how he died is still a mystery. I doubt that he had been another creature's prey. His body is largely intact. Maybe he succumbed to disease or injury.

Or perhaps he just lived out his life. It was surely a good one. Amid the towering pines, he'd have foraged for insects in deep bark crevices, his strong bill hammering, his long tongue slithering down purposefully to capture burrowing prey.

Though alone now in death, this bird certainly had companions in life. He was a mostly solitary fellow, but as dark, winter days grew longer, he'd notice the quivering flight of a female bird seeking a mate. Like the female, he'd extend his neck, point his bill skyward, and bob his head from side to side. Together the birds would flick their wings as they circled a tree trunk, their toes skittering against the rough bark. In the fervor of courtship, they'd chase each other in fast, looping flight through the trees. He'd drum on a tree loudly with his bill to impress her, and she'd return his amorous call. Then, the two birds would become a pair.

Later, in the warmth of spring, the male would drum again to claim his territory. Then, as the sun glinted from the glassy river, he and the female would excavate a deep nest, perhaps in the underside of a dead tree limb, making a bed of wood chips at the bottom. In a couple of weeks, the female would begin laying eggs.

The male hairy woodpecker would have been an attentive parent, hunting for insects and bringing them to the nestlings. He would have been fastidious, too, helping to keep the nest clean and deter predators by carrying off the baby birds' fecal sacs.

Yet, when the busy breeding season ended, he'd leave the female and return to his solitary life, until a certain warm breeze coaxed him to seek a partner once again.

The ways of this bird are not unfamiliar to me. While his smaller, look-alike relative, the gregarious downy woodpecker, mingles easily with its own and other species, vying capably at crowded feeders for bits of suet and seeds, the hairy woodpecker seeks sustenance mostly in quieter, out-of-the-way places. I, too, know this need for space and solitude. I also know the instinct for partnership and devoted parenting, as well as for contented aloneness. In my life, I've taken turns at each. But, unlike me, the hairy woodpecker glided through his life transitions without fear. Without angst. Without suffering. Guided by the seasons, he had a clarity of compass I will never know.

I kneel beside the bird and imagine him in life: his

swift, undulating flight; his powerful foraging; his staccato drumming. Only in death would he allow me so near.

Further up the beach I find a place close to the tree line, where the water will never reach, and dig a hole in the warm sand. I pick up my soul friend and place him gently in the hole. I cover him with sand and place bits of broken shells on top in the shape of a star. In the center, I make a cairn of small stones: white, turquoise, and gray.

I bend down close to the grave and whisper a farewell to the bird.

"Rest easy, dear friend," I pray. "Remember your sweet days in the pines, when the breeze ruffled your feathers and the summer sun warmed you."

As I stand and brush the sand from my knees, it occurs to me that in life, this bird was an insect predator, but now, beneath the ground, he is their prey. It is nature's way. We are all humbled by the grave. Respectfully, however, I keep these thoughts to myself.

The Red-Headed Visitor

It was the rarest of holiday gifts, arriving unexpectedly without ribbons or wrap. There I was, idly eating my Raisin Bran on a chilly December morning—the thirteenth, to be exact—when I happened to look up from my cereal bowl and glance out the kitchen window.

What I saw made me stop midspoonful. My mouth opened wide, but not to consume the cereal. There, amid the leafless limbs just beyond the deck, was a roughly robin-sized bird with a snowy white breast, jet-black upper wings and tail, and a head fully wrapped, from crown to neck, in deep, velvety red. I was seeing for the first time a bird seldom seen in West Virginia: a red-headed woodpecker.

I watched wide-eyed, still open-mouthed, as the bird attempted an awkward and, ultimately, unsuccessful landing on my domed bird feeder, a station more suited to chickadee-sized birds. Finding my feeder completely unaccommodating, it departed hastily, leaving me to watch its swift, undulating retreat. In seconds, it was gone.

Still wondering whether or not to believe my eyes, I left my cereal to get soggy and phoned a couple of

birder friends, who shared my delight. I then flew off the phone to clean my suet cages, which had been languishing in the garage since last winter, and fill them with the commercial cakes that were hiding behind leftovers in the refrigerator. As locally uncommon as the red-headed woodpecker is, I knew that it might be a long time before I would see one again. But perhaps—just maybe—I could woo the bird back.

The red-headed woodpecker is a cavity nester and more adept than most woodpeckers at feeding on flying insects. Thus, it prefers open areas rather than dense woods, and multiple snags for nesting, roosting, and foraging. The bird's range includes most of the United States east of the Rocky Mountains, as well as parts of southern Canada.

The red-headed is among the birds listed on the National Audubon Society's 2002 Watchlist, an early-warning bird conservation system. According to Audubon's website, this woodpecker has experienced a fifty percent population reduction since 1966, due, in part, to food source losses and habitat degradation by harvesting of snags, clear-cutting, agricultural development, and other causes.

According to J. Lawrence Smith, noted state naturalist and historian, and author of *Birds of the Kanawha Valley*, red-headed woodpeckers were numerous across West Virginia in the 1800s. Though their numbers have cycled up and down historically, "it's been downhill all the way for the last 50 years," Smith says. As a breeding bird, the red-headed woodpecker has essentially been gone from the Kanawha Valley since the 1970s. By roughly 1980, a marked reduction in nesting red-headed woodpeckers was noted statewide. Thus, the birds are almost never seen locally in the summer months. Limited sightings have been reported in recent years during spring and fall migration and in winter. Red-headeds

are seen more often in the Eastern Panhandle, but even there they are not common.

Smith believes that, at least initially, the introduction of the aggressive European starling, which vies with the red-headed woodpecker and other cavity nesters, such as bluebirds, for nesting territory, contributed to the red-headed's decline. And while habitat loss has also been a factor, there are places where their habitat has remained unchanged, but the birds have disappeared.

"It's kind of a mystery," Smith says. "It has been hard to get a handle on what is going on."

As it turned out, my attempt to tempt this winter visitor succeeded, for later that day, I spied the red-headed again, this time clinging warily to the side of an oak. As I watched, immobile, the bird flew from its perch in one great swoop, wrapped its toes firmly around the spokes of the suet cage, and began to dine with repeated, determined jabs.

Since December 13, I have observed "my bird" regularly—sometimes several times a day—as it comes for fuel to warm its belly. In the six weeks since I first noticed it, I have learned its predinner flight pattern—no longer a cautious, tree-to-tree approach, but a great swoop from a high branch and a direct landing onto the suet. Because it often announces its arrival in the yard, I have learned its voice—not unlike the red-bellied woodpecker's persistent chuck-chuck-chucking, but more insistent. More staccato. And louder. It calls me away from wherever I am in the house to marvel at its crimson countenance and at how it chose my yard to seek at least some of its winter sustenance.

I have not been able to contain my glee about this and have, short of stopping perfect strangers on the street (Excuse me. Did you know that I have a red-headed woodpecker in my yard?), shared the news with everyone I've seen. People who are not bird lovers smile politely and respond with a quizzical "Oh?" Fellow birders, on the other hand, draw in a sharp breath, while their eyes light up and expressions of utter envy spread across their faces. Their first utterance is not "Oh?" but "Oh!" and it is sometimes followed by "I've only seen a red-headed twice in my life!" or "I haven't seen one in twenty years!" Indeed, it is good to have one's obsession understood.

The day of the Charleston area Christmas Bird

Count, a national event sponsored by the National Audubon Society, my red-headed woodpecker provided the perfect excuse to stay home and bake bread, while still making an important contribution to the count. While ten teams of birders fanned out across the county to places such as Kanawha State Forest, Spring Hill Cemetery Park, Davis Creek, and Coonskin and Ridenour Parks, I measured and mixed, glancing continually out the kitchen window. At first, I saw only the usual suspects: a pert Carolina wren, several American goldfinches, a couple of white-breasted nuthatches, and a pair of downy woodpeckers. But then, about 11:00 AM, I heard that insistent, staccato call and looked up to see the red-headed woodpecker, resplendent in its feathered tuxedo, unseat a starling from the suet. At day's end, of the many teams of birders and feeder watchers participating in the count, I was the only one to report seeing a red-headed.

In the fourteen years I have lived in Charleston, I have thrilled to many bird sightings just beyond my

kitchen window, though none so rare as the red-headed woodpecker. I've seen a pileated woodpecker, the ptero-dactyl-like bird with the magnificent red crest, drop out of the sky like a cartoon superhero, and land on the deck railing. Then, with a mighty hop, it attached itself to the suet cage, where it crumbled the cake with power-ful stabs of its bill. I've seen brilliant yellow goldfinches, rosy house finches, and indigo buntings together light up my cylinder feeder like a springtime Christmas tree. My feeders have even served as a stopover in spring for lovely rose-breasted grosbeaks (the bird on the first West Virginia wildlife license plate), tired and hungry after their long journey from the tropics, and on their way to breeding grounds in West Virginia and places farther north.

I've come to believe that, at least in my neck of the woods, bird-watching reflects one of life's important principles: You never know what treasures you might discover in your own backyard, if you only occasionally look up from your Raisin Bran.

Afterword

Since this essay was first published, I've lived in three Charleston neighborhoods. For more than twenty years, I did not glimpse another red-headed woodpecker in any of them. But then, on February 16, 2024, I looked up suddenly while walking my dog to see a bird with a crimson head in fast flight. In seconds, it was gone. Hoping against hope, I walked home quickly, put Zeke in the house, grabbed my binoculars, and headed back to the spot. Yet, scanning the bare limbs of the old oaks there, I did not find the bird. Nor did I see it the next

morning or the next afternoon. But the following day, I spied it foraging high in an oak snag, the bright winter sun gleaming off its snowy body and richly red head.
From that day on, I walked daily to the little oak grove to see if the bird was still there. It usually took me only a minute or two to find it, as it stayed amid the oaks, flying from snag to snag, foraging peacefully, quietly, and alone.

Weeks went by. Temperatures rose and plummeted, thunderstorms and high winds blew in, and snow squalls swirled. With sunny daffodils and elegant hellebores blooming far below, the red-headed woodpecker scaled hefty limbs and clung to the hollow, hole-ridden snags of the oaks.

While bands of blue jays squawked nearby and pairs of robins chased one another near the ground, the red-headed woodpecker remained a solitary soul, high above

the fray. At times, starlings stalked the bird until it flew to a different tree to avoid harassment, but it always returned. It favored a particular snag with a large hole, likely made by a pile-ated woodpecker. Sometimes it appeared to be excavating a new hole, removing chunks of debris with its powerful bill. Other times it simply perched outside the large hole, as if guarding it, the breeze ruffling its delicate feathers.

In early April, a tornado whipped fiercely through our neighborhood, downing trees and sending a trampoline sailing into another neighbor's yard. Yet the next afternoon, I found the red-headed woodpecker calmly going about its business. Nearly a week later, it was equally unfazed by the near-total solar eclipse that captivated much of the human species in our city.

In these early weeks of spring, nature burst forth in its fervent quest for life. A pair of cardinals began building a nest in a boxwood beside my front door. A mourning dove carried tendrils of dried grass to a cozy place in a neighbor's tall shrub. Two mockingbirds squabbled and chased each other in keen territorial pursuit. I wondered how long it would be before the red-headed woodpecker relinquished its solitary ways and set off in search of a mate.

Then, on April 25, I noticed the bird at the very top of a tree, on a tall, naked branch. Nothing surrounded it but blue sky. Rather than quietly foraging, it was vocalizing robustly, emitting a string of calls, one after the other, almost like a mockingbird. At the same time, it spread its wings and flexed them repeatedly, bobbing it head, then tucking it under its wing and drawing it out, as if it had a powerful itch it could not satisfy.

Was this display a fervent effort to call in a mate, I wondered? Then came the discovery I wished were mine, but it belonged to an astute birder friend and neighbor who, on April 26, spied THREE red-headed woodpeckers atop the same tree where my winter friend had been calling its heart out the day before. The next day I went in search of the trio but did not find them. I heard only a soft "churring" that might have indicated they were still there. The next day and the next, I found no evidence of the birds. I can only surmise, happily, that they flew off together to a nesting colony somewhere, perhaps even one nearby.

These red-headed woodpecker sightings, as well as news of a few other winter sightings of this bird in my region, give me hope that perhaps the red-headed wood-pecker is on the long flight path back to being a more common species. According to *The Second Atlas of Breeding Birds in West Virginia*, the bird was common in the state at the turn of the twentieth century. Yet, after the blight that destroyed nearly all American chestnut trees in the early to mid-1900s, its populations began to decline and sightings became uncommon.

In surveys for *The Second Atlas*, performed from 2009 to 2014, red-headed woodpeckers were observed more frequently in the central western, southeastern, and northeastern parts of West Virginia, and in scattered locations throughout the state, except at the highest ele-vations. While observations were still too few to draw any conclusions about changes in statewide occurrence, in some areas, populations of the bird appeared to have increased since surveys for the first atlas were performed (1984 to 1989); in others, they seemed to be holding steady.

According to West Virginia Division of Natural Resources State Ornithologist Rich Bailey, co-editor of *The Second Atlas*, red-headed woodpeckers "continue to be regularly reported by birders, and certain areas of the state have relatively high numbers, such as the pastures and farm country of the Greenbrier Valley, as well as

North Bend State Park. While data are somewhat sparse, they continue to point to a stable, if not increasing, trend in West Virginia."

Still, the red-headed woodpecker is on the Partners in Flight Yellow Watch List, due, in part, to significant population declines throughout most of its range. Particularly in urban areas, the birds have lost the shelter of cavities in dead trees and limbs, as people have trimmed and removed them. They also suffer predation by sharp-shinned and Cooper's hawks, the populations of which have risen, possibly, Bailey says, from reduced human persecution and exposure to pesticides, as well as increasing urbanization. Yet, the resilient red-headed continues to prove its willingness to adapt to new habitats. The birds have been observed in recent years at golf courses and in mature, closed-canopy forests.

In 2004 and 2024, I enjoyed red-headed woodpecker sightings in my neighborhood all winter long. I will be on the lookout for one amid the little oak grove next winter and hope that sightings like my earlier ones become more and more common throughout this bird's range.

The Quest for the Orange-Crowned Warbler

Most people associate a cemetery with grief and loss. But for bird lovers in Charleston, West Virginia, joy and discovery await at the city's historic Spring Hill Cemetery Park, especially in spring. With its grassy knolls and mix of tall pines and hardwoods, this burial ground teems with avian life, as songbirds returning from the tropics build nests or pause on their way to breeding sites in our deeply wooded hills.

Indeed, so renowned is the cemetery for spring migrants that wildlife biologist Jerry Westfall traveled seventy-five miles from Parkersburg on a recent Sunday morning with one goal in mind: to glimpse the elusive orange-crowned warbler at Spring Hill.

The orange-crowned is a drab little bird but for the

bright patch on its head, for which it is named. Out West, it's common to see this warbler during spring migration. But in West Virginia, it's a rare find. Still, Charleston birder Russ Young saw one at Spring Hill Cemetery Park last year. That was enough for Jerry to rise before dawn and hightail it to Charleston, almost a year to the day of Russ's sighting.

As our band of Sabbath birders walked along the cemetery's open paths, we spied Eastern bluebirds and a sassy brown thrasher. We noted a rough-winged swallow soaring overhead. We heard the mournful whistle of a white-throated sparrow. Between bird finds we chatted amiably, as birders do.

Then, suddenly, Jerry's head cocked forward, his body froze, and all conversation ceased. His brow creased as he listened intently. We all listened. "Hear that?" Jerry asked softly, motioning to a line of trees at the edge of the cemetery. We listened again.

Jerry lived out West for a time, and he knows the voice of the orange-crowned warbler. It's a thin, rapid trill that descends toward the end. Kind of, Jerry said, like, "*Tee-Tee-Tee-Tee-Tee-Tee-Tee-Tee, Too-Too-Too-Too.*"

Jerry followed the sound, and we followed Jerry. Soon we were standing near the trees he had pointed to, our eyes transfixed on their leafy branches. We watched intently for a flit or a hop—trademark warbler behavior.

Now the bird called loudly, leaving no doubt about its identity. Jerry's eyes were round and bright, but then, suddenly, hidden by his binoculars. In that moment all binoculars rose, as did a collective gasp of birder delight.

The orange-crowned warbler had emerged from the leaves, offering us a perfect view. In the morning sunlight, this bird was anything but drab. Though we saw no orange crown, its breast was lemony bright.

Later, Jerry jotted his find in a notebook. His quest had been a great success.

Meanwhile, high above the headstones, the orange-crowned warbler trilled on, each note sounding ever sweeter.

Oaks

*Once a child of the
woods, I fell asleep to the
flute songs of thrushes.*

I am fond of the four oak trees that tower over my next-door neighbor's yard. They are stately but not massive. Judging by their width and height, I would guess them to be about as old as I am.

For years I have watched the oaks in every season. I have seen them in their winter nakedness. Skeletal in the cold, their slim, sturdy limbs are long and winding. With gangly curves and angled elbows, like the arms of ghouls they twist left and right, down to gnarled, spindly fingers.

In winter the oaks look strong, but in their bareness they seem plaintive. Reaching toward the sky, as if in silent supplication, they long for something I cannot imagine. For what do the trees plead? Surely not for peace. Or patience. The oaks are models of these.

In late summer, while the oaks are still lush and green, their acorns become unhinged and hurl themselves to the ground. Some plummet to the hood of my car with a *ping!* Others plop onto my driveway with a *pop!* From there they bounce and roll downhill like bobbling eggs in a race. Prior to impact, or sometimes upon it, they lose their jaunty caps, which also pepper the driveway, looking like tiny wooden bowls for mice or moles.

Soon there are hundreds of fallen acorns in my yard. In the morning air, cool now as fall approaches, I set about gathering them, one by one.

I know there are easier ways to rid my yard of the oaks' countless progeny. Rakes, a broom, buckets and tarps litter my garage. But the scrape and scramble of the rake—a swift sweep—are not for today. I have laid aside the phone and left the laptop sleeping. For now, I wish only for quiet engagement in the company of the oaks.

As I bend to pick up an acorn and place it in my palm, the sun warms my back and dries the dew on delicate strands of grass. Nearby, a white-breasted nuthatch clings upside down to the rough bark of my silver maple, chuckling at the enormity of my task.

But I am not deterred. I reach for another acorn, and another, and another. Against my fingertips they are smooth, cool, and damp with dew. Resting in my open palm I notice their shape, like a woman's breast, curving round to a pointed nipple. I note their earthy shades, like a dusky eye shadow palette, melting from chocolate brown to mocha to caramel. One acorn sports a lovely red stripe. A few are spring green, but those are rare.

By the handful I bring the acorns to a plastic pot, pour them in, and watch them tumble together in a quiet cascade. Meanwhile, others clatter into my neighbor's gutters. The cautious ones land in the soft mulch of my garden bed with a mere, muffled *flumpf.*

I bend and reach again, feeling the gentle pull of muscles in my back and thighs, stiff with the years, ready for release. I bend and gather, carry and pour. Then I begin again. In these moments I want nothing more to do than this.

Meanwhile, the new day unfolds. Beneath a blue, cloudless sky, a ruby-throated hummingbird lingers at the feeder, sipping nectar for its long journey south. I hear the whistling flap of mourning dove wings. Amid a sunny bunch of chrysanthemum blooms, a neighbor's cat licks its elegantly striped belly.

I bend to my task. A red ant and a crow pay no attention. High above in the maple, the nuthatch remains amused.

Must life be unkempt,
unclear, not at all like ants'
journey through tall grass?

The next morning, I pick up the near-full pot of acorns and discover a drama unfolding beneath it. A tiny grub, soft and white, is the subject of intense exploration by a band of ants. The ants—the kind that come for kitchen drippings—are even tinier. Indeed, the grub, though curled into a loop, outsizes the ants many times. It lies seemingly motionless, as the ants travel atop it and around it, like marauders assessing their spoils.

I go back into the house to find a magnifying glass. Moments later I am crouched beside the scene, like Gulliver, peering into a Lilliputian world.

Among the shiny ants there is constant motion. Antennae atwitter, their wiry legs scramble as their pin-

cers probe the pale, lined body of the grub. I see that the grub has a brownish head and pincers of its own. At moments it writhes, stretches slightly, then curls again.

Is the grub dying, I wonder, or is it already dead? Does it move only in a twilight dream, a muscle memory of soft soil and easy darkness? In the glare of the sun its skin gleams.

I watch as eight ants begin to move the grub. Some pull with their pincers; others stand on their back legs and push. In a mere minute or two, they have dragged the grub five inches, up and over a steep, concrete incline imbedded with pebbles, where the driveway curves toward the house. They tug and push, tug and push, in a seamless, unified effort. Like a benevolent deity, I move crisp-dry leaves out of their way.

The ants then pause as they are joined by more ants. The newcomers climb on the grub and walk its length. Others circle the operation. They touch antennae, as if in consultation.

The ants resume their task and proceed to drag the grub perhaps a foot or more, where they lodge it in a crevice at the base of a brick wall.

Here it appears that operations become muddled. The

ants push the grub further into the crevice but then lift it out again. Scores of ants teem under the grub, as others try to push it further into the crevice. Then the ants rock the grub to the left, then to the right, then to the left again, then to the right. It seems that progress has stalled. A curious potato bug cruises by unnoticed.

Meanwhile, above, I have grown impatient. "Why this breakdown in communication?" I ask the ants. "Where is your leader?"

Just then, with a loud "chuck-chuck," a red-bellied woodpecker announces its arrival in the silver maple. Seeking insects, the bird and its kin have bored great holes in the tree's rotting trunk, hastening its demise. Unlike the oaks, the maple is weak. It hasn't much longer to live. Acutely aware of this, the woodpecker turns to its forceful foraging.

"You'd have made fast work of this grub," I tell the bird.

My stomach now rumbling, I find I have the steadfast-ness of neither the oaks nor the ants. I leave the insects to their crevice dilemma.

When I return sometime later, the grub is gone and so are most of the ants. Not willing to bear witness, I can only imagine how the story ends: a feast in the colony, a festive air, a queen well pleased.

Its nipple split, the
acorn presses forth a root,
meaty, milky, strong.

Days later, fog has settled over the ridgetop. It hangs below the trees, perhaps down to the rooftops of cars. The air is cool but not cold. A sweatshirt will do.

In my yard I find the delicate, frayed petals of pink asters clasped tightly together. As the day warms, they will open again. Though it is late in the year, the fresh bouquets of sedum blossoms seem new.

I move to the path beside my house to resume my gathering. Here I scoop up clusters of acorns, hiding like fugitives beneath the slim foliage of irises and liriope. Some, covered with a thin, damp layer of soil, have sprouted thick roots. Others have split open entirely, revealing their hard, cream-colored flesh.

Everywhere intricate spider weavings, caught between tips of grass blades, make fairy hammocks that glisten with dew. I run my hand through my hair and find the damp fog-air nestled there. Does it also coat the oak leaves, still clinging to their branches? Does it shimmer on the iridescent wings of starlings?

> *White-throated sparrow*
> *whistles soft and low, mourns the*
> *passing of summer.*

I have not seen a hummingbird in many days. Now, yellow jackets swarm their near-empty feeder. Along the driveway are three large pots full of acorns. Each day I have gathered, I have left more for the deer and squirrels. If they have partaken, I cannot tell. Perhaps, like me, they prefer to gather their own.

One day the last acorn will fall. I wonder who will witness it? A chickadee or cardinal? An enterprising squirrel? Surely not I.

When the leaves fall and winter returns, I will linger less outside. I will walk by, bundled up, leaving the oaks to their silent prayers. I will return to an interior life, behind glass, and await the bright faces of daffodils, the voice of the wood thrush, the hummingbird's glittering red throat.

Afterword

Since the first publication of this essay in 2017, three of the four oaks have fallen. One was upended in a fierce windstorm that unearthed its gnarled and rocky root ball and swept its great crown to the ground, along with a tangle of powerlines. Though the fallen oak otherwise caused no damage, my neighbor feared the others might one day fall on his house.

Thus, amid the intrepid climbing of workers in cleats, and the insatiable gnawing of chainsaws, limb by leafy limb, two more oaks came down. Much like the ant operation earlier described, men in hardhats crawled on and over the felled trunks, consulting one another, trimming and chopping, until the wood was cut and neatly stacked by the road. Then, one day, it was all carted away.

Some months ago, I happened to step out my front door, turn my head, and watch as a hefty branch of the last oak emitted a mighty crackle and fell to the ground. Thankfully, there were no children or pets beneath it. Some of this oak's limbs hang over another neighbor's driveway. It is only a matter of time before this tree, too, is felled.

These days I have far fewer leaves to rake in fall and hardly any acorns to gather. I see more blue sky. My living room is sunnier. Still, I miss the autumn colors of the oaks, the unfurling of their leaves in springtime, and their stark winter silhouettes. I am glad that this testament to them still stands.

Window Watching

In the grip of the coronavirus pandemic, my small city shutters. We go inside, hunker down, fearing illness and death. We wash our hands and we watch the news. We watch the world outside our windows too. Beyond the windowpanes, impervious to our plight, wild things remain wild. From behind cold glass we mark their comings and goings, having so few of our own. In this troublesome time, they enlarge our shrunken lives.

* * *

On the crowded street where I live in Charleston, West Virginia, houses sit shoulder to shoulder on either side, like twin regiments, and march along a lengthy ridgetop. My road is a busy cut-through between downtown and the town next door. Traffic is continual and rumbles with buses, pickup trucks, and SUVs.

In the early weeks of isolation, my only vista is the one just beyond my living room window, where I've hung bird feeders in the old silver maple that dominates my tiny front yard. As I shelter in place, my companions are mostly feathered—those I can still invite over for suet and seeds.

It's always good to entertain old friends: cardinals, tufted titmice, chickadees, and downy woodpeckers. But when the rose-breasted grosbeaks drop by in early May, it feels like a down-home picnic has become a fancy gala. The birds are elegant: he in his dapper black tux and bright pink cravat, and she in understated earth tones, sporting her signature white eye stripe. I can hardly tear myself away from their company.

While I, along with much of humanity, am grounded by the virus, the rose-breasted grosbeaks and other neotropical migrants keep their travel plans. They leave their wintering grounds in Central and South America, and many fly more than a thousand miles to reach the Gulf Coast of the United States. Some days after making landfall, six stunning male grosbeaks arrive in my silver maple.

There've been springs when I've not seen a single rose-breasted grosbeak at my feeder. At best, I've noted one or two that stayed a few days. Usually they rest and refuel briefly before continuing further north to their breeding grounds.

But this year, for nineteen incredible days, I lift my window shades just after dawn and see a grosbeak, or two or three, already poised on the feeder, stocking up on black oil sunflower seeds. After the third day, the otherwise empty blocks on my calendar begin to fill with exclamations.

"RBGs still here!!" I write on Day 8. "2-3-4 at a time on the feeders!"

"3 males at 9:30 AM!" I note on Day 13.

For nearly three weeks, I host a daily reception, keeping the buffet stocked and watching the revelers mingle. Behind the window, I am but a wallflower, relegated to observing the dramas and dynamics.

Unlike confident resident birds, grosbeaks do not fly directly onto the feeders. Instead, they land in the leafy branches above, glance around, gauge the competition, and then descend. Once they are feeding, they are unfazed by rumbling vehicles, human voices, yapping dogs, and growling lawnmowers.

The resident birds accept the newcomers graciously. The grosbeaks, however, are a bit aloof, if not aggressive. Grosbeak males will sometimes lower their heads toward a male cardinal cousin and nudge him off the feeder. Equally brazen, a female grosbeak does the same to a downy woodpecker. Grosbeak males also vie with each other for space at the feeder, jockeying for position, sometimes fluttering off but returning quickly.

It is common to see a male cardinal gallantly offer his mate a seed. Not so the grosbeak male. On the contrary, I see them nudge their female counterparts off the feeder. The females take it in stride. Apparently used to their mates' boorish behavior, they wait on a nearby branch for their turn.

Yet, a male grosbeak will, at times, defer to a territorial cardinal or raucous blue jay. Both can unseat him handily from the feeder. There are also the crass party crashers, with whom the grosbeaks do not mingle: the pack of mousy gray, juvenile starlings that commandeer the suet cage in open-billed squabbling, and the squirrel that drapes itself, like a fur stole, over the feeder, prohibiting any avian diners.

While I marvel at my great fortune in hosting the grosbeaks for so long, I also wonder why there are so many of them and why they have not moved on. Bird behavior is complex. Our state ornithologist says birds surely take cues from temperature and food availability. He speculates that this year, a weather event may have driven more of the grosbeaks to migrate through the Appalachian region instead of through other areas of the country. Then, our cold springtime temperatures likely slowed their progress northward. They stayed a while longer where food was abundant. Indeed, the birds' adaptability and resourcefulness seem all the more amazing in this time of human fragility and uncertainty.

On the twentieth day since the grosbeaks' arrival, I lift the living room shade ever so slowly and peek out at a gray sky. Glancing at the feeders, I find a lone, male cardinal, his hefty bill busily working a sunflower seed out of its hull. I gaze out for a long while. Titmice, chickadees, and house finches come and go.

But where is the glamour, the flair? After several more checks at the window throughout the day, I know the rose-breasted grosbeaks have moved on. I feel as if I have been left to sweep the floor, take down the streamers, and gather up the empty champagne flutes. Indeed, the party is over, and I will have to wait a whole year to host another one.

Yet, after a time, I glance out the window and see an elusive flicker, with its scarlet nape stripe and polka-dotted breast, stabbing the suet cake with gusto. Before long, a brown thrasher with flashy yellow eyes arrives, bringing a brood of two. I watch a male downy woodpecker feed dabs of suet to his nestling. And, oh! There is an impish hummingbird buzzing in for nectar.

My ears awaken to the seesaw notes of a yellow-throated warbler and to the wood thrush's captivating flute melodies. Both of these migrants nest in little patches of woods near my home. Though I never see them, their songs sweeten the air well into summer.

* * *

Along with warmer temperatures come spikes in coronavirus cases. Safe behind my window, I watch not only birds but also passersby. There are more of them now: people jogging, walking their dogs, strolling their babies. I watch my Facebook feed, too, and check daily posts on the neighborhood page. There, on an evening in late June, I make a startling discovery: a video of a black bear lumbering along a busy, nearby street. The animal looks confused as it crosses the parallel, yellow lines in the middle of the street and then stops to consider a guardrail. After a time, a hefty pickup truck comes up the street. The driver sees the bear, which is now out of our view, and slows to a stop.

The video ends there, but the next day, neighbors post more, and photographs too. I see the bear lifting the lid of a trash can and eyeing the bulging, white bags inside. Later, it helps itself to birdseed. Sitting in the grass, it grasps a neighbor's tubular feeder with both front paws and brings it to its mouth, like a small child drinking a glass of milk. Then I watch the bear handily scale a chain link fence, lifting its rump and short back legs to the top, and then bounding over to the other side.

As residents of a heavily wooded state, my neighbors and I are used to white-tailed deer meandering through our yards and, unfortunately, decimating our gardens. I've seen a young buck wander up my driveway. Once I counted five does, each with a fawn, ambling peaceably together, browsing grass and leaves.

But a black bear in the neighborhood? That's news. In fact, the local TV news features our bear, making it a bit of a celebrity.

At first, my neighbors are amused by our big, furry guest. One posts a picture of Smokey Bear, standing tall in his blue jeans and ranger hat, solemnly grasping the handle of his shovel. Another adds an image of Yogi Bear in his porkpie hat and necktie, making off with a picnic basket. Indeed, our bear is soon dubbed "Yogi."

"Hey, Boo-Boo!" another neighbor quips, referencing Yogi Bear's loyal sidekick. This time the bear can be seen walking up a driveway toward a white SUV.

"He's up here enjoying our Red Lobster leftovers!" a nearby neighbor reports one evening.

"Tomorrow's trash day," yet another notes. "The bear should have a great time!" His post is accompanied by an emoji laughing to the point of tears.

Yet, I, for one, cannot join in the jocularity. Seeing West Virginia's official state animal, a magnificent, woodland creature, amid cars and gas grills, reduced to

picking through trash cans, makes me sad.

Shortly after the bear's arrival, my neighbors notify officials at the Division of Natural Resources (DNR), who instruct us to secure trash cans and bird feeders, and to bring pet foods inside. A bear that continues to find food will become a nuisance, they caution. Bears habituated to human food can be hard to relocate and must be euthanized. A fed bear is a dead bear, we are warned. Not wanting to attract the bear to my yard, I reluctantly take down my bird feeders.

A DNR biologist informs us that our bear is a male yearling, a young bear recently turned away by his mother, who is preparing to breed again. Wandering our neighborhood, then, is a misguided, ursine adolescent, getting into scrapes while trying to find his way. Who among us doesn't have a story or two like that to tell? My heart aches for him.

It is rumored that the DNR will set a trap for Yogi, and, because he is a yearling and weighs only about one hundred seventy pounds, relocate him to a state natural area. But a couple of weeks go by and that doesn't happen. It's hard to say why. In the midst of the pandemic, everything has slowed down. Everyone is struggling. I try to cultivate patience and expect less.

Meanwhile, the bear is reported within a block of my house. Though I never see the bear, a dark-green scat in my backyard leaves me wondering. Thereafter, while working in my garden, a twig snap or leaf flutter sends me whirling around, scanning the tree line. Though there are no reports of Yogi bothering people or pets, I stop walking my dog after dark.

As time goes on, my neighbors become less enamored of the bear. Nerves fray and tempers flare on Facebook. One person speculates that the DNR may be overwhelmed and suggests we raise money to hire a private company that deals with nuisance wildlife to relocate the bear.

"Don't kid yourself," another replies. "That bear can't be saved. It's been up here too long. They'll just kill it and say they relocated it. Why should we pay for that?"

The retort: "And who pissed in your Cheerios this morning?"

All the while, Yogi roams our streets, eventually expanding his territory. A neighbor some distance away opens her door at five in the morning and startles him from her porch. He runs to her magnolia tree and climbs it. Not long after, he is seen enjoying breakfast at the dumpster at the neighborhood swimming pool.

Finally, after nearly three weeks, the DNR tells us they are coming for the bear. Sightings have become so frequent and communication so rapid among neighbors that the biologists do not need a trap. Near dusk, they drive to the yard where the bear has been seen minutes before. They find him, tranquilize him, and load him into the bed of a pickup truck. Destination: a twenty-three-thousand-acre natural area some seventy-five miles away, featuring an oak and hickory forest and a trout-stocked lake.

* * *

With the heat of summer upon us, the rose-breasted grosbeaks are long gone, and so, now, is Yogi. Though I am glad the bear's life was spared, I know he is not yet out of the woods, so to speak. Hunting black bears is legal in our state and allowed in the area where he was set free. Still, for now, I imagine him roaming beneath a leafy canopy, remembering the lessons he learned from his mother, peacefully foraging for roots and berries, fungi and insects.

Meanwhile, the rest of us carry on. We don our masks. We keep our distance. We bundle our bags of trash and ply paved streets, sometimes slowing to allow the deer to cross.

A Quiet Committee

I stand at the kitchen sink, washing my hands yet again, when out of the corner of my eye I see a dark shape soaring outside the window. It quickly disappears from sight but then returns, a hulk-ing mass flying toward the trees. I watch intently now as it rears up, unfolds expansive wings, and lands in near-bare branches. The bird is now unmistakable.

"Turkey vulture," I say out loud, as I dry my hands with a damp towel. I've used the towel several times today already. I glance down at my hands and rub them, feeling their sandpaper roughness, noting the raw, bright-pink peaks of my knuckles.

When I glance up again, I see two more enormous birds join the first one; one sidles up on the same branch, while the other settles on a limb nearby.

"How about that," I say to myself. "A meet-up of vultures."

I know these birds like to gather in groups. So do I, but right now, I am not allowed to.

Indeed, due to the COVID-19 pandemic, I'm alone a lot more. I also have more time on my dry, chapped hands. I cannot see my friends, but a visit with vultures is still permitted. I go to find my binoculars.

Peering through the lenses, I see tree branches just beginning to sprout. The tender, lime-green leaflets are so small, I can see the birds easily between them.

I find the trio and zero in for an up-close view. Hunched and homely with heads hung low, they grasp the branches with long, pink toes. Their feet are the color of my knuckles, and they match the birds' pulpy faces, which I imagine look not unlike the entrails they pull from a roadkill opossum or raccoon.

I wonder why they have chosen to gather in my tree. Is there something dead just over the hillside? A deer? Pray not the gray cat that skulks through my yard each day. Neighbors tell of coyotes howling in the night, though I have never heard one. Anyway, a coyote would surely make off with its prey, not leave it.

A quick, online search informs me that a group of perching vultures is called a *committee* or, if they are feeding, a *wake*. I eye them again. With their heavy heads in a close, dark huddle, they look like mourners. Yet, I learn that, rather than congregating near something dead, the birds may be migrating and just stopping here for a rest.

While I am enthralled with the vultures, two blue jays

are not. They mob the larger birds, diving toward them relentlessly, hopping up and down in the surrounding branches, cawing loudly in alarm.

"It's OK. They're not hawks," I reassure them. "They won't steal your babies."

Still, the jays carry on, while the vultures roundly ignore them.

I watch as the big birds settle in. One lumbers along a smooth branch, sidestepping awkwardly, as if feeling for the most comfortable spot. Another flexes its unwieldy wings in a wide, cumbersome stretch, then tucks them neatly next to its body. The third lifts a wing and dips its head beneath it, perhaps preening away a bothersome mite. In all this, I notice the birds' easy familiarity with one another, perhaps the kind I have with close friends who know my idiosyncrasies and love me just the same.

I think now of those friends who, like me, are largely isolated in their homes. I think of my children, who live far away. How long must I wait to see them, feel the comfort of their smiles, hug them tight? In this moment I envy the quiet company the vultures keep with one another.

I am reminded that these birds are no strangers to death, nor are we in this troublesome time. Indeed, one unshielded breath could lead to our last. And if we succumb, there can be no wake or other service where loved ones gather to mourn us. I am grateful to be safe inside, waiting it out, if alone.

I watch the birds for a long while and then return to my solitary tasks. Under a cloudy sky, backyard life goes on. Squirrels skitter up trees and take no notice of the dark heaps in the branches. A Carolina wren sings loudly. In the distance, a tufted titmouse calls insistently for a mate but gets no reply. The blue jays give up and go about their business.

May 2020

... It was
another day in my history of posthumous
days, another day when nobody touched my body.
—*From "Stained" by Irene McKinney*

I wake in the night and find my dog stretched across the bed. Curled on my left side, I occupy but a sliver of mattress. I get up to use the bathroom and when I return, I cannot nestle in without nudging him.

"Move over, pal," I say softly, pushing him gently with my knees. As I turn over, he stands for a moment, then curls down against my body, his back pressed to mine. In minutes we are both asleep.

In the morning, I find him stretched parallel to me, his head resting on my thigh. Bleary-eyed, I rise up on one elbow.

"Good morning, Murph," I say. "How's my sweet potato? How's my sugar boy?"

His warm, brown eyes brighten, and his tail thumps the covers soundly, like a woman in the old days beating dirt out of a carpet.

Sitting up, I stroke his head and then bend to bury my face in the thick, soft fur around his neck.

"You smell good," I tell him, and he does, like baked earth and spring grass. I rub his paws, lifting one to my nose. It is warm. It smells good, too, like toasted nuts.

I rub his belly and tug on the floppy triangles of his ears, feeling their velvet softness on the tender skin between my fingers. I turn his ear flaps over, where the skin is bare and pink, like peony petals, and plant a kiss on each one.

In that moment I am a little girl again, with my arms wrapped around the neck of Scotty, a small, black dog who was supposed to be a Scottish terrier. That's what his owner told my father. In fact, Scotty was more of a rat terrier, we learned, and he had bad habits, like chewing dirty laundry left on the floor, especially underwear. But I loved him all the same. I called him Lover Boy.

"Stop kissing that damn dog," my father told me time and again. My father worried. It was an era of scarlet fever, measles, and, God forbid, polio. Who knew how children contracted these dreadful diseases?

Now, more than ever, I understand my father's fear. Still, I do not—cannot—stop kissing the dog.

* * *

Global: 4,342,565 cases; 296,690 deaths
National: 1,389,935 cases; 84,059 deaths
West Virginia: 67,110 tested; 1,404 positive; 64,330 negative; 59 deaths
        —The *Charleston Gazette-Mail*, May 14, 2020

Some mornings I wake with the startling knowledge that I have not been touched by another person in weeks. Every cell of my body cries out for it, a keening at dawn. I was in a relationship, but it ended before all this began. I am no stranger to being alone, but always before, there were close friends to hug hello and goodbye. There were warm kisses on the cheek. There were spring visits to my daughter's house, when we planted impatiens and geraniums in bright pots, drank coffee, and talked while our dogs played in the yard. There were visits with my son when we talked for hours over a beer or two. He helped me paint and move furniture, and then we talked some more. Always I could wrap my arms around my children and my children-in-law, and feel the comfort of their arms around me.

"I mourn these precious times we will never regain," a friend writes in an email. Her father is 96 and sheltering in place with her brother on the farm where she grew up. She longs to see his smile, sit on the front porch swing, and hear the music of the nearby creek.

"Me, too," I write in reply.

* * *

"Dr. Anthony Fauci, the nation's top infectious disease expert, plans to issue a stark warning to the Senate this morning over the dangers of reopening the country's economy too swiftly. Fauci said ... that doing so could result in 'needless suffering and death.'"
—The *New York Times*, On Politics, May 12, 2020

A friend of a friend has died, not from the coronavirus but from brain cancer. I'd met him on several occasions. He was a warm, engaging man. He always had a smile. Doctors told him that only one percent of those with his cancer survive.

"I will be in that one percent," he told the doctors. He was a very successful businessman. He knew how to aim high.

But in the end, he fell short. Because of concerns about the virus, his family was not allowed at his bedside until the very end.

I sit quietly on my couch and absorb the sad news. My sacrifices shrink in the wake of bitter cruelties others endure.

* * *

"As more virus research has emerged, the outdoors has begun to look safer … Besides the research, something else has begun to make the outdoors seem more attractive. People have started to go stir crazy. This combination is leading to a surge of new expert advice that might be boiled down to: Get out."
—The *New York Times*, The Morning, May 14, 2020

My friend Martha calls and says she is in town just overnight. She invites me for a hike with our friend Midge. "I'd love to go," I say, "but we'll have to socially distance."

"Whatever," Martha replies.

I've known Martha a long time. She lives more dangerously than I do. She lets her dogs lap leftover gravy and sauce directly from the pans. She pays little attention to food expiration dates. She pulls tall poke weeds out of her yard and sautés and eats them. Her husband does not partake.

Once, years ago, when Martha still lived around the corner, I called her at four in the morning because I was afraid I was having a heart attack. Deep down, I knew I wasn't, but I needed reassurance. I needed someone who would not be filled with fear and tell me I should go to the emergency room—now.

In minutes, Martha was at my door. She made us both a cup of tea. She sat with me on the couch until dawn came and my stress pains left. She made me feel I could trust myself.

"Sometimes a cup of tea and a friend are all you need," she said, her arms open wide.

* * *

What is all this juice and all this joy?
—From "Spring" by Gerard Manley Hopkins, SJ

And now we are in the woods, three old friends and our dogs. Martha chose this trail because she knows larkspur blooms here. Walking single file and rarely six feet apart, we spy the rosy-red, starlike blooms of fire pink, nestled near the ground amid the leaf litter. Midge uses her walking stick to point out sorrel, its tiny, pink-purple flowers rising above clover-like leaves brushed with blood-red trim.

May apples cover the forest floor, some in showy,

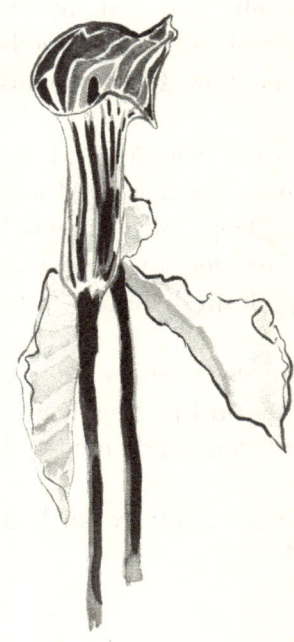

snow-white bloom. Others display the tiny, green, oval-shaped "apple" for which the plant is named.

Hiding in the shade, amid a trio of broad, green leaves, is a stunning jack-in-the-pulpit with deep-maroon stripes. I say that Jack looks jaunty, as he peeks out from beneath the flap dipped rakishly over his head. Midge and Martha laugh.

In a way, the forest makes us giddy, like children. Hearing the voice of an Eastern towhee, Martha and I lift our heels up and shuffle back and forth, mimicking the way the bird rustles up leaf matter while foraging on the ground. We laugh some more.

As we walk, the woods ring with wood thrush flute song. The calls of an Eastern wood-peewee and a red-eyed vireo can barely be heard amid the loud pronouncements of Carolina wrens and cardinals.

Then, as the trail dips down, we find larkspur in abundant bloom. Each flower has a long spur at the back that reminds me of a witch's hat, or perhaps a unicorn horn. Indeed, the blossoms are every bit as magical.

Close to two hours later, having forgotten about the virus, we emerge at the trailhead. We do not tarry. Martha has a long drive home. We pause for but a moment, exchange conspiratorial glances, and then hug one another. Our embraces feel clandestine, and they are all too brief.

"If people see us, they'll say we're crazy," Midge says. "We're breaking the law!"

But there are no witnesses, only a rose-breasted grosbeak offering its sweet, fluid song from the branches of a towering beech.

What Seasoned Birders Taught Me

With spring's arrival in West Virginia, throngs of neo-tropical migratory birds return to our forests, parks, and neighborhoods to breed. In celebration, I rise each morning just before dawn, strap on my binoculars, go outside, and fire up the Merlin app on my smartphone. Together, Merlin and I listen for the voices of birds newly returned to my neighborhood. Just this morning, unbeknownst to me but quite apparent to Merlin, Tennessee and bay-breasted warblers, as well as an American redstart, were singing brightly in the tall, old oaks and maples around my house.

When I began my love affair with birds many years ago, there was no such thing as an app for identifying them, let alone a smartphone on which to open it. In those days, novice birders relied on experienced ones, who helped them recognize birds by their field marks, behavior, voice, and location. Group outings and weighty field guides were the best ways to get to know birds. Rather than tapping or swiping phones, we huddled together, elbow to elbow, binoculars aimed at a tree or tangle, our own voices hushed to hear the avian ones.

The quest for elusive birds bonds those who share the passion. There's a deep connection you won't make with the rectangular microcomputer resting in your palm. For me, those outings have not only forged lasting friendships but provided vivid images that inform my birding life to this day.

When I hear the mournful whistle of the white-throated sparrow, I think of Ken, a veteran birder who, years ago, taught me that the bird's vocalization sounds like "Poor Sam Peabody, Peabody, Peabody." Its soft song soothes me on cold winter mornings, when few other birds are singing.

When I see a sleek gray catbird or hear its insistent "mewing," I think of Marilyn, who first pointed out the bird to me. As it emerged from a thick cluster of magnolia leaves, she noted its slim silhouette; chic black cap; and elegant, slate-gray plumage. The catbird is a mimic, she told me. Like the mockingbird, it copies the songs of other birds and sings them, one after the other.

Marilyn also taught me that the scarlet tanager sounds like "a robin with a sore throat," and that the white-eyed vireo says "Pick up the beer check!," or "beer, chick!," if you loosen your birder decorum. And while Marilyn showed me the chipping sparrow's "rusty ball cap," it was Cindy who taught me that this bird makes a sound like "the whirring of your grandmother's treadle sewing machine."

Birder friend John told me that the male house finch looks like he's been "dipped in strawberry juice." He also told me I could remember the trill of the Northern Parula warbler by imagining someone running fast up a flight of stairs and then jumping out a window. The image still makes me smile and helps me remember this bird's zippy call.

More experienced birding companions also taught me patience. Once, on a forest trail, our leader, Russ, waited many minutes for a hooded warbler to emerge from a tangle of vines. We watched and waited, watched and waited, listening to the bird call "wheat-a wheat-a wheat-e o," until it finally emerged from the thicket. Like a Met Gala star posing on the carpet, it perched before us, stunning in its bright yellow plumage and black cowl. This was the first warbler voice I memorized, likely because I witnessed the little bird singing, its wide-open bill thrown skyward above its bobbling throat.

While some longtime birders are reluctant to use technology, relying instead on their own sharp skills, many others use Merlin to confirm, enhance, and report their avian findings. Merlin can be handy for older birders who have lost the ability to hear the soft *zpee* of a blue-gray gnatcatcher, the high-pitched pick note of a downy woodpecker, or the soft flute song of the wood thrush. While many older birders mourn the loss of their hearing, it seems certain that Merlin's auditory powers will only improve with time.

Indeed, Merlin's ability to identify birds by sound, as well as other characteristics, makes it a powerful teaching tool. After my morning listening sessions, I can return to each recording again and again to hear the avian voices, which light up when Merlin hears them.

There is no question that Merlin and eBird, its companion reporting tool, both developed by the Cornell Lab of Ornithology, are revolutionizing citizen science and our understanding of bird populations and locations. According to the Cornell Lab's eBird Monthly Recap, in April of 2024, more than 140,000 birders worldwide contributed more than two million checklists, with more than 29 million bird observations, to eBird.

Yet, as technology advances avian conservation and education exponentially, gatherings of companionable birders will never become obsolete. On a recent walk in Spring Hill Cemetery Park, a favorite birder haunt, I watched our leader, Russ, cup his hands around his ears, making them mini-satellite dishes, to home in on one avian voice. He listened intently for a long moment before declaring the presence of a Kentucky warbler. The Kentucky's was the first of many warbler voices Russ recognized that morning.

Later, through steadied binoculars, he scanned the thick, gleaming limbs of a giant sycamore, listening to the call of a brown thrasher. The rest of us scanned too, until Russ finally exclaimed, "Ah, there it is!"

His sharp eyes also drew our attention to a soaring black vulture, a bird not common in these parts; a red-tailed hawk circling in the sun; and a yellow-breasted chat, which emerged briefly from a scrubby thicket.

Walking on paved paths amid the headstones, Russ then spied a bush weighty with plump peony blooms and recalled a time, long ago, when he snipped one and gave it to a young woman he was "sweet on."

"I think this would look lovely behind your ear," he told her. Charmed, Russ's crush took the flower and clipped it into her hair. Moments later, she yelped and began madly brushing at her neck and shoulders.

"Ants," Russ told us. "The peony was full of ants."

"Oh, no!" we all cried.

"Aw, too bad!" someone said. "That's how love goes sometimes."

Russ nodded and smiled. Then, amid a cool spring breeze, we went back to quietly walking and scanning the tree line.

Believers

On the day of my mother's funeral, I lay awake long before dawn, in a spare room of her home, my mind drifting to painful scenes from the last several days: my mother lay in her hospital bed, still and waxen-yellow, her small frame covered in a clean, cotton gown dotted with tiny, blue flowers. A nubby, white blanket is tucked beneath her arms, their loose skin mottled with crimson and purple blotches. The oversized, hose-like tubes in her nostrils that had rushed oxygen to her lungs the night before are gone. In place of their urgent shushing is silence.

I sit beside my mother, talking to her softly through tears. I bend to kiss her forehead, something I never did when she was alive. I feel the coolness of her skin and breathe in a trace of soft scent—lotion or afterbath powder.

Then, my thoughts shift to my mother lying still amid the satiny, cream-color cushions of her casket. A deep-red mahogany, accented with delicately carved flowers, the casket is elegant. My siblings and I chose it after agreeing it looked more feminine than the others.

Mom is wearing the tailored black suit with the white piping she chose for the occasion. Earlier, I feared the suit would look too dark, too grim to be Mom's last fashion statement. She had a flair for color and style. It was important to Mom to look beautiful.

In the days leading up to her services, I worried that the funeral director would not do my mother justice, that she would not look like herself for her last gathering of friends, and that I would be embarrassed for her. My sister and I had picked out black-and-silver earrings to match her suit. I brought them to the funeral home, along with one of her favorite lipsticks, her eyeglasses (the funeral director said if you wore them in life, you should wear them in the casket), and a picture that showed her beauty and how she wore her hair.

When the time came for her viewing, I came prepared. In my purse I had tucked another lipstick and one of Mom's hair picks, just in case. On the arm of my daughter and with my son close behind, I approached the casket with trepidation. Reaching the edge of it, I cautiously peered down. More like a scrupulous product inspector than a grieving daughter, I eyed my mother critically. With carefully applied makeup, her skin tone had returned to creamy beige. Her hair was styled the way she would have liked, except for the bit of gray that was showing at the roots. Her hands were positioned peacefully atop one another on her belly, highlighting her nails, newly painted a tasteful raspberry pink.

Indeed, resting amid the casket's pillowy lining, my mother looked all of a piece, as pretty as a corpse could, I thought.

I finally took a breath. Then, I knelt down beside my mother and touched her arm. It felt rock hard and cold beneath the soft cloth of her suit. I leaned in close to give her my report.

"You look beautiful, Mama," I whispered. "They did a good job."

For weeks following my mother's death, I would call up this image of her sleeping in the casket with her glasses on. It felt like the only reliable evidence I had that she was, in fact, dead.

* * *

As I lay in bed in the mid-December darkness, reliving moments that felt unreal, a loud, intrusive sound outside the window pulled my attention away. The sound was clipped and repetitive. I wondered if it would wake my children and their spouses, all of whom were sleeping in rooms adjacent to mine.

Though mysterious, the sound was not entirely unfamiliar. I'd heard male cardinals make their *chipping* sound many times, as they prepared to feed, scoped out nesting territory, or signaled to a female warming a nest.

This sound was akin to chipping, but there was something disconcerting about it. Normal cardinal chipping is measured and moderate: "chip ... chip ... chip ... chip ..." This bird, if it was a bird at all, was making a loud, rapid-fire, almost frantic sound: "CHIP! CHIP! CHIP! CHIP!"

The racket continued unabated as I got out of bed and went to the window. I separated the vertical blinds and peeked out. There, just steps away, high atop the crape myrtle, was a cardinal, its slim body and handsome crest silhouetted in predawn light. As I looked on, it continued to chip its heart out.

"What's going on?" I asked the bird. I scanned the yard and sky briefly for any cause for alarm—a skulking cat, a perching hawk—but saw none. What was the reason for these persistent vocalizations, except to draw me from my bed in wonder?

Just the morning before, I had gone to the funeral home to drop off some memorabilia to display at Mom's visitation. I had gathered a wedding picture of Mom and Dad; a memory book filled with photographs and messages from family members, which we had presented to Mom for her ninetieth birthday just ten days earlier; and a thick binder of newspaper clippings and other keepsakes from Mom's successful real estate career.

I handed them to the funeral director's assistant, a kind woman who admired each one. In turn, I admired the pin she had nestled in her scarf, a handsome male cardinal perched in pine boughs.

"That's so pretty," I said, nodding toward the pin.

"Thank you," the woman replied. After a moment she added, "You know, when you see a cardinal, it means a departed loved one is nearby."

Her words made me pause and catch a breath.

"My mother believed that," I told her. "But I didn't know anyone else did."

"Oh, yes," the funeral assistant said emphatically.

"They're around here all the time," the funeral director confirmed, motioning toward the window and the expansive, green lawn beyond it. "They're always out in the yard."

Indeed, earlier in the year, after the untimely death from cancer of her beloved niece, my cousin Elizabeth, my mother said she saw cardinals in her yard more frequently. She felt sure they were a sign from Elizabeth, who was sending her love and reassurance. Though I was glad my mother was comforted by the birds, I was skeptical. It was summer, after all, and seeds and insects were abundant in her yard.

But now, in the chill of winter, here was a cardinal, right outside my window, calling loudly and more insistently than I had ever heard one call before.

Later that morning, sharing coffee in my mother's dining room, I asked my daughter if she had heard the cardinal. She said she had not, likely because she uses a white noise machine to help her sleep. I told her about the insistent chipping at dawn, my conversation with the funeral home staff, and her grandma's belief that cardinals were spiritual messengers.

"Maybe that was Gran outside our windows, sending

us love and telling us she is in a good place," I suggested to my daughter. She nodded and smiled a little.

"I want to believe that and so I will," I added.

I wanted my daughter to believe it too. She loved my mother dearly. The two of them shared a deep bond born of their playful, childlike natures. Of course, in the beginning, my daughter *was* a child. As she grew, she found in her grandma a most beloved playmate, her "first best friend," she once told me.

Dress-up was one of their favorite games. My mother would provide accessories from her own collection and others she'd find at yard sales: hats, wigs, scarves, dress gloves, jewelry, purses, and high heels. My daughter would don them and prance around, creating a personality to match each outfit. This delighted my mother, who loved nothing better than to interview my daughter's chic, eccentric characters. It became my daughter's mission to evoke my mother's laugh, which was unreserved and could shake a chandelier.

My daughter and my mother also sang and shopped together. Their favorite departments were lingerie and hats. My mother would try on a flamboyant chapeau and then stand still with a bemused expression, waiting for my daughter to turn around and see her. The end result was peals of laughter. At ten years old, my daughter would try to outdo my mother's silliness by trying on Dolly Partonesque bras over her clothes. She'd pose seductively, hands on hips, eyes toward the sky. This reliably undid my mother.

Years later, their dress-up days long passed, my mother remained my daughter's best audience and biggest fan. She applauded loudly at dance recitals, karaoke performances, and graduations. The two still enjoyed occasional shopping trips and still could not resist silly hats.

Yet, in recent years, my mother's failing health slowed her down considerably. She became sad as her world began to shrink. Though she had lived nearly a century, she wondered aloud what she had to show for it.

My daughter buoyed her up, reminding her of her heady days in real estate and the clients who admired her, as well as the many other people she touched and delighted throughout her life. My daughter was among them, and she lovingly let my mother know this.

* * *

Back in the dining room, my daughter and I kept our conversation brief. The funeral was in just a couple of hours. There were two bathrooms and six of us to wash and get ready. My daughter also needed to type the Bible passage about love from St. Paul to the Corinthians—a favorite of my mother's—which she would read at the funeral. I left her sitting at the dining room table, tapping on my laptop.

A while later, I returned to the dining room to show my daughter the elegant, black blouse I had found at a local department store just a few days earlier. I had stood wearily amid racks of pricey, picked-over clothing, trying to tune out strains of the seductive "Santa Baby" and the peppy "All I Want for Christmas Is You," while anxiously looking for anything black in my size. Spending hours happily perusing racks of clothing was something I did with my mother through the years. Now, in the store, I felt the enormous weight of her absence. Yet I could almost feel her holding me close, comforting me as I went about my sad errand. I couldn't help but feel that she pointed me directly to the attractive, seven-dollar blouse that went perfectly with the pants I already owned.

As I entered the dining room holding the blouse, I saw that my daughter was no longer at the table typing. She was standing with her back to me in front of the glass doors to the backyard. When she turned, I saw that her face was streaked with tears. She motioned to me to come to the door. I stood beside her and put my arm around her shoulders.

"Look," she said, pointing to the tall elm my father had planted and nurtured from a sapling. The two of us looked up into the great tree's bare crown. Perched in the branches were perhaps a dozen cardinals, holding silent vigil in the gray light, even as a bitter-cold rain began to fall.

I looked in amazement at the birds. I knew that cardinals sometimes travel in winter flocks. But in all my life, I had only seen one. Now, here they were, high above my mother's house filled with her mourning children, just hours before her funeral.

My daughter looked at me then, her eyes glistening. We stood for a long time, saying nothing, holding one another, beholding the birds. Neither of us had any doubt who had sent them.

Nature's Constancy

In the quiet near-dawn of a bitter January morning, a distant twittering grows louder and louder, until I am called to my front door to look outside. I arrive in time to see scores of American robins descend into the holly tree that occupies much of my front yard.

Suddenly my tiny yard is abuzz with the burbling whinnies and chuckles of a frenetic flock of robins. Filling the tree with a flutter and flap of wings, they send a shower of snow dust sprinkling to the sidewalk as they pluck berry after bright-red berry. In their feasting fervor, some perform a flutter dance from branch to ground and back again. Others, rosy and plumped against the cold, await their turn from telephone wires and the bare branches of a nearby elm.

For many moments I stand transfixed, watching the resourceful birds forage cacophonously against a backdrop of an otherwise subdued morning. I wonder where they roost at night and how they survive these frigid temperatures. I marvel at the adaptability of this bird, which lives as easily in the city as it does in the forest. When worms and insects are not available, it lives on berries and fruits. And for a nest, the umbrage of a well-traveled front porch does as well as a secluded, leafy tree.

I am lost in thought until I notice the sudden return of quiet. The birds leave as swiftly as they came. Before long, I hear only their distant twittering. The holly tree stands empty, stripped of berries. And in the plain light of day, the yard is once again still and silent.

The calm, often drab days of January signal a new calendar year, unbeknownst to the plucky robin, or, for that matter, to the great blue heron, standing regally at the banks of a gray-green river, rippled by frosty winds. Neither does nature know of the turbulent year we leave behind, a time of economic downturn, when the stock market, riding the tide of human emotions, resembled a woodcock mating dance, spiraling high into the sky, only to zigzag dizzily back to earth.

Indeed, as we begin a new year, we do well to remember the trusty robin. It is good to seek the beauty of a waterfall's icy glaze, or the exquisite pinstripe of the puttyroot leaf, peeking out from beneath the snow. Particularly in the midst of tumult, the constancy of nature offers unfailing comfort.

Acknowledgments

Many of these essays have been previously published and appear together here for the first time.

"From Poetry to Prose" was first published in *The Brevity Blog* on January 15, 2020.

"May 2020" and "A Quiet Committee" (under the title "Wake") were first published in *In the Midst: A COVID-19 Anthology*. Collection Copyright 2020, Sandy Tritt, editor.

"Nature's Constancy" was first published in *Wonderful West Virginia*, Vol. 73, No.1, January 2009.

"Oaks" was first published in *Voices on Unity: Coming Together, Falling Apart*, Mountain State Press, 2017.

"The Quest for the Orange-Crowned Warbler" was first broadcast on West Virginia Public Radio on May 11, 2014.

"The Red-Headed Visitor" was first published in the *Charleston Sunday Gazette-Mail*, February 1, 2004.

"Window Watching" was first published in *Stonecrop Review*. Issue 4: Fauna, 2021.

Bibliography

Bailey, Richard S., and Casey B. Rucker, eds. *The Second Atlas of Breeding Birds in West Virginia*. University Park: The Pennsylvania State University Press, 2021.

"Coronavirus numbers," *Charleston Gazette-Mail, May* 14, 2020.

Russonello, Giovanni, "Where things stand," On Politics, *New York Times*, May 12, 2020.

Hopkins, Gerard Manley. *The Poems of Gerard Manley Hopkins*. Edited by W. H. Gardner and N. H. MacKenzie. 4th ed. London: Oxford University Press, 1970.

Kacian, Jim, Philip Rowland, and Allan Burns, eds. *Haiku in English: The First Hundred Years*. New York: W. W. Norton & Company, Inc., 2013.

McKinney, Irene. *Vivid Companion*. Morgantown: West Virginia University Press, 2004.

Leonhardt, David, "The new 'get out' push," The Morning, *New York Times*, May 14, 2020.

Cornell Lab of Ornithology, *eBird Monthly Recap*, April 2024.

In Gratitude

I have learned that it takes the skills and generosity of many to write a book. I am grateful to all those who helped me make this dream come true. They include writer and artist Colleen Anderson, my longtime mentor and friend, who read every word and offered gentle advice and strong encouragement; Missy Woolverton, whose skillful editing and proofreading, as well as loving support, greatly improved the manuscript; Una Karner, who, on long walks, expressed delight and affirmed and encouraged my dream; and writers Laura Treacy Bentley and Cat Pleska, fellow members of my Trillium writers group, who offered invaluable critiques and helped facilitate the first publication of several of these essays.

I am also indebted to West Virginia Division of Natural Resources State Ornithologist Rich Bailey, who is always available to answer my bird questions, and who so generously read these essays for scientific accuracy; writer and teacher Rebecca McClanahan and my fellow students at Wildacres Retreat, where I workshopped the essay "Selving" so many years ago; naturalists Beverly Wright, Marjorie Keatley, and John Northeimer, who read and listened to my work, encouraged me, and shared their deep knowledge of the natural world; and Nora Shalaway Carpenter, Laura Boggess, Cindy Ellis, Dan Day, Nancy Buckingham, Sara Crickenberger, Terry Pickett, and Al Peery, who shared my excitement and helped nudge this book out into the world.

My deep appreciation also goes to the Blackwater Press team: Vivien Williams and Samantha Stafford for outstanding proofreading; Luca Guariento for his artful design and typesetting; and Elizabeth Ford, who welcomed a proposal for a book of nature essays, and who, just minutes into our first conversation, visualized what you now hold in your hands.

I am also grateful to illustrator Sophie Kromholz for her artistry and sensitivity. Only with the addition of her striking drawings did this book become what it was truly meant to be.

When I was a young mother, I let my children know often that I was proud of them. I didn't know that many years later, I would want them to be proud of me. This book is also for my children and children-in-law, Megan and Josh, and Patrick and Alison, who listen, know me, and encourage my dreams. And for Myles Jack, that he might discover nature and love it all his life.

And finally, I am greatly indebted to my canine beloveds: Scotty, Shamrock, Seamus, Murphy, Missy, Zeke, and Lucy, who have walked beside me throughout my life, as they do throughout these pages, offering unlimited love, loyalty, and devotion.

About the Author

Writer, editor, and naturalist Sheila McEntee's essays have been featured in *Stonecrop Review*, *The Brevity Blog*, *Still: The Journal*, and *Woods Reader*, among other publications, and on West Virginia Public Radio. Sheila wrote for *Wonderful West Virginia* magazine for many years, and from 2006 to 2014 was that publication's editor. Raised in Cheverly, Maryland, and Hingham, Massachusetts, she is a graduate of the College of the Holy Cross. She lives in Charleston, West Virginia.

Visit Sheila McEntee online at sheilamcentee.com.